Seeds of Success
A Handbook for Young African Americans

By Vernon Arrington Jr.

The Deluge Press
Egg Harbor, New Jersey

Published by The Deluge Press
P.O. Box 657, Egg Harbor, NJ 08215-0657

Cover design by IMAGIC Digital, Cardiff, NJ
Typography by LY Designs, Nashville, Tennessee

Printed by Vaughan Printing

ISBN 0-9642493-0-8

Ask how your church or social group can make a difference by distributing *Seeds of Success*. For details, call The Deluge Press at (609) 965-7407.

Printed in the United States of America

INTRODUCTION

Seeds of Success is a special book with an ambitious objective. If it achieves its intended purpose, not only will it help improve the lives of our young people, it will save lives. Its aim is to inspire maturing young African Americans to higher levels of achievement by encouraging a greater degree of personal expectation and commitment. For young men and women with unanswered questions about how they might shape and direct their futures, *Seeds of Success* may be the most important book they will ever read. If the members of this generation are to prosper from the development of their enormous potential, we must instill in them individually the character and the will to relentlessly explore that potential. It is imperative they understand that the course of their futures will be determined by how well (or how poorly) they apply the principles of self-discipline, self-motivation, and self-reliance. If we cannot provide them with a clear understanding of what success will require, we have failed them.

Seeds of Success was so named because it contains 228 vital messages of inspiration, instruction, and enlightenment. If cultivated, these messages, like seeds, will grow to enhance the lives of those who are receptive to them. This book's definition of success has little to do with money or income levels. More appropriately, it defines success by how effectively one can establish and accomplish goals, negotiate obstacles, resolve problems, and handle responsibilities.

This small handbook could become a big factor in expanding the prospects of young individuals who make it their objective to succeed in life. A valuable resource, its messages will inspire compelling and constructive dialogue between parents and children, students and teachers, friends and acquaintances.

You can help spread the *Seeds of Success*. Whether you purchase this book for yourself, a family member, or someone else you care about, it could be the most profitable investment you will ever make. For all of us in the African-American community who are genuinely concerned about finding solutions to the difficult challenges confronting us, *Seeds of Success* is a decisive step in the right direction.

For innumerable reasons,
this book is dedicated to my mother and father.

Special thanks
for the gracious contributions of
my wife Sharon, son Bryan, daughter Lindsey,
Alice Cash, Pam Cross, Felisberto "Tot" Maceia, Tyleesha Brantley,
Kathleen Flatley, Danya Kraft-Stolar, Morris Taylor,
Kathleen Nelson and William Nelson.

Thank You God for Your divine guidance.

Through these windows,
may you have a broader view of life's possibilities,
visualize your objectives and aspirations,
and better see the path that leads you to them.

stamp or signature

*This copy of **Seeds of Success** was made*
available through the efforts of the above
organization or individual.

1. Wake up in the morning with a sense of purpose. Lie down at night with a sense of accomplishment.

2. Remember your mistakes and learn from them.

3. Learn from the mistakes of others; it's less costly than learning from your own.

4. Be resilient. When life knocks you down, get up fast, get up stronger, get up smarter.

5. Work for the things you want; never expect them to be given to you.

6. Don't squander a good opportunity; you may only get a few in your lifetime.

7. Don't be intimidated by how difficult a task appears. Failing is not the worst thing that could happen—failing to try is.

8. Develop a thick skin. Hold your head up and keep trying no matter what others do or say to dissuade you.

Be undaunted.

9. As for your detractors, success is the sweetest revenge.

10. To have the least advantage is to have the greatest potential.

11. However difficult it may be, listen to those who offer constructive criticism; it may be the most valuable help you'll ever get.

12. BE RESOURCEFUL.

THE SECOND BEST THING TO HAVING ALL THE ANSWERS IS KNOWING WHERE TO FIND THEM.

13. Great personal achievements only result from sustained goal-oriented effort.

14. A strong body isn't much of an asset when coupled with a weak mind.

15. Compete as vigorously in the classroom as you do in the sporting arena.

16. Strategy...execution...determination...
     mental toughness...desire...quickness...
     concentration...

     The attributes that are common among
     winners in the sporting arena also
     define winners in the game of life.

17. Be a keen observer and a focused listener.

18. Don't underestimate anyone.

19. You're a lot smarter than you realize, and more intelligent than others will ever give you credit for being. Continually challenge yourself to learn.

20. While you have little or no control over the behaviors and attitudes of others, of greater importance is that you have control over your own.

21. No one has more power and influence over your life than you do. A strong individual is his own best friend, a weak person, his own worst enemy.

22. Consider the opinions of people whose views differ from yours; their impressions may help to broaden your perspective.

23. If average people use less than 10% of their mental capacity, how much are you using?

24. While it is the school system's responsi-
     bility to give you an education, it
     cannot do so unless you have first
     realized your responsibility to get an
     education.

25. In life there are limits to how far you
     can go, but only by reaching, stretching,
     and extending yourself will you ever
     know what those limits are.

26. If you're a high school student who wants to attend college, you would be wise to begin your inquiries early in your sophomore year.

    Aggressively enlist the help of your parents, teachers, guidance counselors, clergy, and other adults who have an interest in your future.

27. Contact the registrar's office of your target colleges and universities to ask for registration packages, scholarship information, and financial aid availability.

Your grades and your SAT or ACT scores will be the most important criteria for acceptance. Work hard to make them reflect a strong commitment to further your education.

28. Select a major course of study after careful deliberation. Know that you can reconsider your decision and pursue a different major if your interests change; many students do.

Your freshman year in college will be the most critical. A high percentage of first year students flunk out because of their failure to exercise self-discipline.

29. When making a career choice, base your decision on genuine personal interests, not on unrealistic dreams of financial reward.

30. Instead of saying "You know what Um sayin," say exactly what you mean.

Well-developed verbal skills are a priceless asset.

31. Being street smart may be useful in many situations, but it won't be the kind of knowledge that gives added value to a résumé or a job application.

Don't waste your intelligence and your ambition on dead-end pursuits.

32. Your greatest opportunity is the chance to discover your own potential. No one should be more curious about it than you.

33. Push yourself. Take a serious shot at being the best. Once you've experienced what it's like to excel, you won't be satisfied with doing less.

34. If you've described other African Americans who strive for excellence, success, and a wider range of experiences as trying to "act White," ask yourself what behaviors you would describe as "acting Black."

It is not always the limitations that others impose on us that hinder our chances for success. Too often, the limitations are self-imposed.

35. THERE IS NO ONE WAY TO
BE BLACK.

RESPECT THE INDIVIDUALITY
OF OTHER AFRICAN
AMERICANS.

36. No one's opinion of you is of more consequence than your own. Low self-esteem and lack of self-respect are the makings of those most likely to self-destruct.

37. Don't sell yourself short; others will readily buy into that notion—without your help.

38. Success is not reserved for other people.
It can be yours to earn. If you can
develop goals and work enthusiastically
toward their completion; be undeterred
by difficulty and resistance; and be
diligent, disciplined, and committed
enough to sacrifice immediate gratifica-
tion for long-term aspirations, success
can be yours.

39. Love yourself. Don't look to others for approval or validation. Your self-image is far too important to allow anyone else to define.

40. If you've dropped out of school, it's never too late to return. If you're considering dropping out—don't. You'll be making the right decision.

41. Although college may not be a realistic
     option, education can still be a priority
     in your life—if you choose to make it so.
     Make learning a life-long experience.

42. Keep a dictionary close at hand.
     Whenever you don't know the
     meaning of a word you see or hear,
     look it up.

43. Study the actions of others: familiarize yourself with the behaviors that make for their successes and the conduct that results in their failures.

44. Voice your opinion; it matters.

45. Value time; it's a limited resource.

46. Respect your elders. Seek out their advice. Profit from their wisdom.

47. Don't use profanity. Build your vocabulary.

48. Be careful what you do or say in the presence of children; they will be quick to emulate you. Set the right example.

49. Complaining about your life won't change anything. Get up and do something about it.

50. It's a fast-paced world. Opportunity falls to those who know what they want and will act quickly and deliberately in taking the initiative.

MOVE.

51. Don't expect a level playing field. In the real world, an equal opportunity is a rare occurrence. Develop your confidence and your competence; it's the only sure way to even your chances for success in a very competitive environment.

52. Even while the opposition rests, the shrewdest and most effective competitors are still at work.

53. It takes little courage or imagination to blindly follow others. People with real vision and insight will forge their own paths.

54. EDUCATION: the empowerment to accomplish things of which you otherwise could only have dreamed.

STAY IN SCHOOL.

55. Large-scale tasks require cooperation. Great things can be accomplished when you and others lend your skills, energy, and ideas to worthy causes.

56. Opinions don't solve problems. Knowing what needs to be done is no substitute for doing what needs to be done.

57. Don't adopt a "get over" mentality. By lying, cheating, stealing, using or hurting other people to win an advantage, you will have lost much more than you could ever gain.

58. The value of trust is difficult to measure—until trust is destroyed.

59. THERE ARE MANY REASONS WHY YOU SHOULD RESPECT AND ABIDE BY THE LAW.

Of the more than 1.25 million people held in State and Federal prisons at the end of 1999, 46% were Black.

THAT'S OVER 570,000 REASONS.

60. When faced with a legal challenge, don't dismiss the need for proper representation. Do yourself a favor, obtain a lawyer—one who specializes in your area of need.

61. Choose your friends carefully; they should be the people who bring out the best, not the worst in you.

62. While in school, become a member of an academic organization, sports team, social club, or one of the many special-interest or activity groups seeking interested recruits. Experience the rewards of participating in a shared commitment and a common cause.

63. Don't be willing to do or say anything simply for acceptance. Show your integrity.

64. Alcohol and drug abuse are open invitations to the living hell of substance addiction. Once you've surrendered control of your life to drugs or alcohol, you may never get it back.

65. Those who sell illicit drugs, broker in the destruction of our families and our communities.

Don't defend them.

Don't support the lifestyle.

66. Death...violence...crime...dependency...incarceration...broken families...wasted lives...

How much has the sale and use of illegal drugs contributed to the health and well-being of your community?

67.   A good way to improve your standard of living: raise the standards you live by.

68.   Develop a habit of evaluating your personal circumstances and what steps you can take to improve them.

69.   Handle problems as soon as they arise;
      they only get bigger and more complicated
      the longer you choose to avoid them.

70.   You will often encounter people who, by
      their words and actions, imply that they
      consider themselves superior to you. This
      will only become a problem if you begin to
      believe them.

71. Young African-American women who have children out of wedlock risk a life of hardship and dependence. Deprived of the advantage of two fully committed parents, children born out of wedlock are far more likely than children of married couples to be born into poverty.

Your children deserve a better start.

72. HIV and other sexually transmitted diseases...teenage parenthood...abortion... abandoned children...the continued cycle of poverty...

The consequences and the complications of sexual irresponsibility are severe. Too many promising futures have already been destroyed by personal recklessness. Don't undermine yours.

73. A well-supplemented education is free. It is as close as the nearest newspaper, news magazine, dictionary, encyclopedia, world atlas, or many of the thousands of books available in your local libraries.

Knowledge is real power.

74. Computers are such an integral feature of most work environments that any student who hasn't learned to utilize them will be at a distinct disadvantage as a prospective employee.

75. The Internet provides easy access to a vast information resource that can improve your quality of life. Get connected.

76. Don't believe that all news reported in print, on television, or over radio is absolute truth. Maintain a healthy degree of skepticism.

77. Learn how to write an effective business letter. It's an ability that will add a valuable dimension to your communication skills.

78. By using illegal drugs, you risk the same
fate as countless other African Americans
whose lives have been impaired or
destroyed by substance abuse. Choose
a healthier diversion.

79. Drug testing is being used increasingly as
a screening procedure for job applicants
and current employees. Stay clean.

80. Your character and judgment will be tested often. Doing the right thing won't always be easy. The distinctions between right and wrong aren't always clear. Trust your conscience.

81. A good reputation is a status that can't be bought—it can only be earned. Become known for your credibility.

82. Take part in the political process. Vote. Important decisions are being made that affect you. You should have some input.

83. Make positive contributions to your community. Stay informed about important community affairs. Become involved.

84. Don't quit, run away, or make excuses when life becomes difficult. Be assured: throughout your life, you will be faced with difficult challenges.

Have the courage and inner strength to accept and face the challenges head-on.

85. BE STRONG-WILLED AND DETERMINED. NEVER GIVE UP.

PERSEVERE.

86. If you believe that the finer things in life are beyond your reach, they probably are.

87. Don't be resentful of people who have more than you do. Take stock in the things that you have, and consider them the foundation on which you can build an admirable life.

88. Never mistake good manners and
     common courtesy for signs of weakness;
     they are indicators of strength of character.

89. Be big enough to apologize to the people
     you have wronged.

90. Ask questions; most people are willing to
     share what they know.

91. Homicide is a common cause of death among young African Americans. Of all the challenges you'll have to face, the biggest may be to live peacefully among your peers.

92. If we do not place a high value on our lives and the lives of other African Americans, who will?

93. Don't seek to solve your arguments by
     using a weapon. Taking a life, or losing
     your own, is too great a price to pay to
     settle a dispute. Violence will compound
     a problem and leave a situation worse
     than it began. The true test of strength
     is not learning how to take life, but
     learning how to live life.

94. Nearly 1 in 3 African-American males between the ages of 20 and 29 are in prison, on parole, or on probation. Too many are making the wrong choices in life, with dire consequences for our families and communities.

The key word is *choices*. Make yours more meaningful ones.

95. Don't pass off your responsibilities to other people—handle them yourself.

96. Don't put your future in jeopardy. You can't protect or provide for anyone else unless you can first protect yourself. For those who need you and depend on you, learn to recognize and avoid compromising situations.

97. Raising children is a parent's fundamental responsibility—one that too many young African-American males are unwilling to accept. Can we expect that our children will live their lives with discipline, self-respect, and accountability, if as fathers, we fail to teach or to demonstrate those qualities?

At what cost has the role model forsaken his role?

98. AN AFRICAN-AMERICAN FEMALE CAN BE THE GREATEST OF MOTHERS TO HER CHILDREN.

SHE CAN NEVER BE A GOOD FATHER.

99. Take a long drive out of the neighborhood once in awhile—there's a much bigger world out there.

100. Read a local newspaper every day. Become familiar with the dynamics of your community. Lack of awareness is a disabling condition.

101. Talk is cheap. Ultimately, you will be measured by your actions.

102. Question the intelligence of anyone who glorifies a life of crime; it's a contemptible, antisocial occupation with an enormous failure rate. The nation's prisons are overcrowded with unsuccessful career criminals—there's no future in it.

103. Being in the right place at the right time
is more a matter of conscious effort than
luck. Only fools leave their futures
to luck.

Ambitious, self-motivated people make
their own breaks.

104. Don't drive while intoxicated. The
     penalties in most states have become
     so severe that a conviction could result
     in your incarceration, thousands of
     dollars in fines, loss of driving privi-
     leges, and much steeper insurance rates.
     Drunken drivers risk their lives and the
     lives of others, often with tragic results.

     The consequences aren't worth the risk.

105. One lie usually necessitates another, and another, and another. The truth will never complicate your life.

106. Organization is a necessary prerequisite to success.

107. Have a résumé prepared and keep it up-to-date.

108. If you have no job, no job is beneath you.

109. Whatever your job, learn it well; skills are very transferable.

110. Arrive on time for work and for appointments. Lateness indicates an individual's lack of preparedness and dependability.

111.   It's normal to experience some anxiety when facing a new challenge; let it be a reason to prepare well.

112.   Before a job interview, find out as much about the employer and the position as you can. Anticipate the questions you'll be asked and be prepared to ask pertinent questions of your own.

113. A job interview should be viewed as a highly competitive situation. If you haven't come well groomed, suitably dressed, and ready for the challenge— you haven't come well prepared.

Assume that all employers will be selective in their hiring process; they're paying—they have a right to be.

114. Value work for what it is: (1) The chance to meet financial obligations, (2) a way to acquire valuable skills and knowledge, (3) a means of achieving long-term personal goals, and (4) a way to experience the pride of personal productivity.

115.　Volunteer work in your field of interest is a good means of gaining experience and making valuable career contacts.

116.　Spend some time browsing through a local bookstore.　You'll likely discover new subjects that interest you.

117. Without the self-discipline to take orders and follow directives, you may never be qualified to give orders or issue directives.

118. It is pointless to be a star performer at work and an underachiever at home. Be willing to work as hard for your personal goals as you do for the goals of your employer.

119. Take pride in your work; it says a lot about the kind of person you are. Take pride in your home—for the same reason.

120. Enjoy your life. Think of it as a gift.

121. Once in awhile, find out what you're missing. Treat yourself and someone special to a fine dining experience.

122. Attend parent-teacher conferences and demand that your child respect all teachers and school administrators.

123. Don't relinquish your role as a parent and expect your child's teacher to fill that void.

124. Treat African-American women with dignity and respect. They have held our families together even in the absence of male heads of households.

125. Promote mutual respect among African-American males. Our common experience should be what unites us—not what divides us.

126. Make charitable contributions to local shelters for the homeless.

127. Support organizations that use their resources to make your community a better place to live.

128.   Respect the institution of marriage; it is the wellspring of strong families.

129.   There is no greater responsibility for parents than taking care of their children, and in doing so, there is no greater fulfillment.

130. Don't be too modest. Your best efforts could go unnoticed and unrewarded. If you won't stand up and take credit for your contributions, someone else will.

131. Don't discuss personal problems with co-workers; some won't hesitate to use your confidence to undermine your standing in the workplace.

132. If you're fortunate enough to gain a substantial cash windfall, bank it until you become rational enough to determine how it can best be used.

133. Money spent well can buy you happiness.

134. Money spent foolishly can buy you lifelong regret.

135. Your employment record will follow you from one job to the next. Your past references can be a great help or a severe hindrance.

Don't damage your future employment prospects by burning your bridges.

136. There are big opportunities available to those who are prepared. You are only limited by your degree of knowledge, curiosity, imagination, and drive.

137. Don't feel discouraged or defeated because a few doors have slammed in your face—try them all.

Persistence pays.

138. MISERY LOVES COMPANY—and so does mediocrity. Don't be swayed from your goals by those who feel threatened by the prospect of your success.

STAY FOCUSED.

139. Think—consider your alternatives. There's always a least and a most effective approach to handling any problem.

140. Many great ideas have yet to be conceived. One could be yours. Keep your mind open to new possibilities.

141. Your life isn't over because you've made serious mistakes. Making mistakes doesn't mean you're stupid—just human. It is stupid, however, to make the same mistakes over and over. You'll have enough obstacles to overcome—don't trip on your own feet.

142. Working smart and planning carefully are the real secrets to success.

143. When budgeting your money, make your <u>wants</u> secondary to your <u>needs</u>.

144. For one month, collect receipts for all of your purchases. At the end of the month, take a close look at how your money was spent. You may need to make some critical changes.

145. Don't be a sucker for "something for nothing" deals. They can be very expensive.

146. If you're not a disciplined saver (like most people) and your employer offers a savings or long-term investment plan through payroll deduction, use it.

147. Never sign a document without reading and understanding it first.

148. Always check your payroll stubs and understand the purpose of every deduction.

149. Don't be quick to throw away personal documents that seem only marginally important.

150. Purchase a file system for important bills and papers so that they can be organized, retrieved, and reviewed when needed.

151. Minimize your credit spending. Pay by cash or check whenever possible. Recovering from excessive debt can be a slow, difficult, and painful process.

152. Use credit cards with restraint. Handled properly, they can be effective tools for establishing a good credit history; misused, they are easy ways to generate serious debt problems.

153. When you learn to say *no*, you'll have learned to avoid some of life's most difficult problems.

154. Unless you're willing to accept the burden of someone else's unpaid debt, avoid co-signing a loan application.

155. When making major purchases, remember: the best price doesn't always mean the best deal. Carefully consider all the terms of the sale before signing an agreement.

156. Don't make a habit of borrowing money from friends and acquaintances. If you do, pay up.

157. Never think of a car as a status symbol.

158. When buying a car, compare the dealer's financing terms with those offered by other lenders. Don't buy from any dealer who is unwilling to fairly negotiate a price.

159. As an African American, borrowing money for a home or a business venture will (to say the least) be a challenge. Expect your credit-worthiness to be strictly scrutinized.

When denied equal access to funding, we are denied equal access to the vast array of opportunities that require it.

160.　Strengthen your chances of successfully borrowing money by: (1) Maintaining a stable employment record, (2) minimizing your debt load, (3) paying bills on time and in full, (4) clearing-up any pre-existing credit problems, and (5) applying to as many lenders as it takes to secure the financing you need.

161. Make your children smarter consumers by having them handle some of your routine purchases. Insist that they compute the final cost and the amount of change to be refunded—before making a transaction.

162. Teach your children the value of getting receipts for their purchases.

163. As soon as your children begin to earn money, assist them in establishing and managing their own bank accounts.

164. Never pass up the chance to show your children how special they are, and how much you love them. A parent's approval is critical to a child's developing self-image.

165. CIGARETTE SMOKING: one of the most preventable causes of death and life-threatening disease.

166. Find healthy outlets for the negative stresses and tensions in your life.

167. Have a good understanding of the total benefits package available to you and your family through your employer. A health benefit that goes unused benefits no one.

168. Don't use cost as an excuse for not seeking treatment for a health concern.

169. Medical problems left untreated will only become worse. Early diagnosis and treatment save lives. Don't let uninformed suspicions and irrational fears become a threat to your continued good health.

170. Stand up for what you believe in—even if it means you must stand alone.

171. The good advice you give to others will also work for you.

172. Never feel ashamed or embarrassed to ask for another explanation of something you didn't understand the first time.

173. Follow through with your commitments. Reliability is a respectable quality.

174. When making important suggestions or complaints at work, submit them in writing. Well-written correspondence is difficult to ignore, misunderstand, or misrepresent.

175. Don't be paralyzed by self-doubt. Everyone experiences periods of uncertainty; keep a positive outlook and work through them. Activity is more productive than idleness. Optimism will serve you better than pessimism. Self-assurance will propel you further than apprehension.

176. TREAT OTHER PEOPLE IN THE SAME MANNER THAT YOU WOULD WANT TO BE TREATED.

It is the simplest, most effective contribution you can make to a better society.

177. Appreciate the qualities that distinguish you from others. Don't abandon them to conform to the superficial media interpretations of how you should think, look, or behave. When you love yourself for your own unique and special character, the real you becomes much more appealing.

178. Make financial contributions to African-American colleges and universities. They have given many of us opportunities and direction.

179. For every step someone is willing to make on your behalf, be willing to make two on your own.

180. Don't destroy someone else's dreams
      if you lack the courage or the will to
      pursue your own.

181. When a problem proves too difficult to
      handle alone, don't be afraid to ask for
      help.

182. If you have trouble remembering,
      develop a habit of writing yourself notes.

183. A love for reading is one of the greatest gifts you can give to a child.

184. Visit your public library. An invaluable resource is available to you and your family—free of charge.

185. Take your children to museums; little minds can handle big concepts.

186. A verbal agreement and a handshake won't secure a deal—get it in writing.

187. When paying for a service, be specific about what you want. Leaving your requirements open to interpretation will mean that your expectations have little chance of being met.

188. Beware of people who solicit your financial investments and contributions by phone. Don't cave in to high-pressure sales tactics. You can say no, or you can hang up.

189. Become a student of African-American history. Few lessons will give you a better sense of pride and perspective.

190. In matters of importance that involve documents, make copies.

191. When a photocopy will suffice, don't surrender an important original document as a requirement of proof.

192. Buy the works of African-American artists and authors.

193. If your employer offers free voluntary training courses that will enhance your skill level, take them.

194. If career advancement training is made available in your workplace, request it.

195. Develop a work record that makes you a prime candidate for promotion.

196.   Don't be tolerant of injustices that occur in your presence. Make your objections known.

197.   With the possible exception of your lawyer, be reluctant to let others speak for you when you are capable of speaking for yourself.

198. ONE BLACK MAN'S OR BLACK WOMAN'S SUCCESS IS A SMALL TRIUMPH FOR ALL OF US.

199. Racism and discrimination are inescapable hazards for all Black Americans. Don't allow them to be the controlling influences that dictate your capabilities in life. The greater the opposition, the more resolute you must become. Achievement and prosperity are within the reach of those who refuse to be denied them.

200. Be objective in your dealings with people of other races. Allowing your perceptions to be poisoned by racial stereotypes or prejudice will only limit your capacity to relate to others.

Gratifying relationships are built on common interests and mutual respect.

201. The strength of the African-American community lies in keeping our families intact. A strong family unit is the basic support system that too many of us do not have.

202. Preserve your family's history by saving video recordings, photographs, documents, and objects of personal importance.

203. Prepare your children well for school. If they start behind, they're more likely to stay behind.

204. Help your children with their homework.

205. Give your family the benefit of information technology. Get a personal computer; the advantages can't be overstated.

206. Because you will not likely find it out-
side your door, keep peace in your house.

207. Don't allow a quick temper to cause
you to commit an act you'll regret later.

Think before you act out of anger.

208. If you want to be a parent and cannot have children of your own, consider adoption. There are thousands of African-American children who need the security of a stable home, love, and the commitment that a real family provides.

209. Reward your children for excellence and for improvement. Extraordinary effort and performance should be recognized and appreciated.

210. Have your children give some of their discarded toys and used clothing to less fortunate children in your community.

211. Don't be the kind of person who takes everything and gives little or nothing. Selfishness is a grim destroyer of personal relationships.

212. Resist the urge to dwell on painful past experiences. You cannot change the past. Turn the page and get on with your life.

213.   Believe in the power of prayer to change your life's circumstances. It is the solution to many difficult problems, the way around seemingly impassable obstacles, and the key to doors of opportunity.

Amen.

214. Don't become so self-involved that you fail to see how much the people in your life need you—or how much you need them. Keep the lines of communication open in your family.

Take time to talk.

215. A poor start in life doesn't have to result in a poor finish. Some of the most successful people in the world started with little more than a sense of optimism and an awareness that their own efforts would be the most important factor in determining the outcome of their lives.

216. When you finally realize the success that you've worked so hard to achieve, don't forget about the people you leave behind. In the same ways others have influenced you, there are those who could be encouraged and inspired by your accomplishments.

217. Because every generation stands on the shoulders of the last, what we do with our lives takes on a greater importance. The opportunities that are available to us exist because of the commitment and sacrifices of our predecessors. We have everything to gain by keeping alive their commitment to progress, and everything to lose if we don't.

218. When we refuse personal responsibility, abandon our faith and sense of purpose, and turn bitterness and frustration into acts of selfishness and self-destruction, we only succeed in accomplishing what 250 years of enslavement could not.

219. Take pride in America; it is as much yours as anyone else's. Despite our many grievances, African Americans have contributed much to make this country great—even when there were few incentives. We must continue to contribute our share if America is to be fertile ground for our children and grandchildren.

220. Think big. Start small. Be willing to crawl before you walk.

221. Set goals, aim high, work hard, and believe.

222. Develop patience. Some goals can only be reached one small step at a time.

223. The Creator has provided you with the most powerful resources imaginable: an inquisitive and reasoning mind, a capable body, and a sustaining spirit.

224. Regardless of what others might expect of you, expect the best of yourself.

225. Take control and set the terms and conditions of your own life. Fail to take control, and those terms and conditions will forever be defined by others.

226. At the very least, pull your own weight.

227. You are not in this alone. Be someone's inspiration—not someone's liability.

228. Be steadfast in your commitment to your goals and to your growth. You were born to accomplish great things. Let nothing, and no one, stand in your way.

*The following pages contain
statistics that outline the realities of
life for African Americans today. While
the information provides an accurate collective
overview, it cannot tell your story or dictate
your chances for success. You have
the power to shape that reality.*

POPULATION

There are characteristics unique to the Black population of the United States. Nearly 60% of us live in the South, and the majority of African Americans live in metropolitan areas. We are a relatively young people with a median age seven years lower than that of White Americans. Since 1980, our numbers and our percentage of the total population have gradually increased. Although our infant mortality rate and life expectancy have improved, the figures still compare unfavorably to the rest of the population.

According to estimates by the U.S. Bureau of the Census, the Black population of the United States exceeded 35 million in the year 2000 and constituted 12.9% of the total population.

Of all Black Americans, 47% are male, and 53% are female. Half of the Black population are older, and half are younger than the median age of 29.8 years.

Source: U. S. Bureau of the Census, Resident Population of the United States: Middle Series
Projections, 1996 - 2000

In 1980, the average life expectancy for a newborn Black child was 68 years—for a White newborn, 74 years. By 1998, those figures had increased to 71.5 years and 77 years respectively.

In 1998, the life expectancy of a newborn Black male was 67.8 years—for a Black female, 75 years.

Sources: U.S. Census Bureau, Statistical Abstract of the United States: 1999, Table No. 127
National Vital Statistics Report, Vol. 47, No. 25, October 5, 1999

In 1998, the infant mortality rate (deaths of infants under 1 year per 1,000 live births) for African-American infants was more than twice that for White infants.

The mortality rate for Black infants was 14.1 per 1,000 live births compared to 6.0 for White infants.

Source: National Vital Statistics Report, Vol. 47, No. 25, October 5, 1999

In 1997, the three leading causes of death for all Americans were, in order, heart disease, cancers, and stroke. In the same order, these were the leading causes of death for the African-American population.

That year, accidents, diabetes, homicide and legal intervention, and HIV infection were the 4th through 7th leading causes of death for African Americans.

Source: National Vital Statistics Reports, Vol. 47, No. 19, June 30, 1999

Despite significant declines in the death rate from HIV infection, AIDS remained the leading cause of death for African Americans, ages 25 to 44, in 1997. For all Americans of that age group, AIDS was the 5th leading cause of death.

For African Americans, age 15 to 24, homicide and legal intervention was the leading cause of death in 1997. Blacks were 8 times more likely to die of homicide and legal intervention than Whites of that age group.

Source: National Vital Statistics Report, Vol. 47, No. 19, June 30, 1999

Of the more than 1.86 million people held in the nation's prisons and jails at midyear 1999, 44% (nearly 820,000) were Black.

African Americans are 6 times more likely to be incarcerated than White Americans, and based on current rates of first incarceration, 28% of Black males will enter State or Federal prison during their lifetime.

Sources: Bureau of Justice Statistics, Criminal Offender Statistics, Prison and Jail Inmates at Midyear 1999, Prisoners in 1998

EDUCATION AND EMPLOYMENT

Since 1980, a greater percentage of young African Americans have been graduating from high school and entering and completing college. The results have been significant. More are being employed as professionals, and those who earn college degrees (on average) have incomes that are substantially higher than those with only high school diplomas. Further improving the employment outlook is the recent economic upturn that pushed 1999 unemployment rates for Black Americans to a record low.

In 1975, 43% of Black Americans age 25 and over had completed 4 years of high school or more. By 1998, that statistic had improved to 76%.

By comparison, the number of White Americans age 25 and over who had at least completed high school was 65% in 1975, and 84% in 1998.

Source: U.S. Census Bureau, Statistical Abstract of the United States: 1999, Table No. 263

In 1975, 6.4% of Black Americans age 25 and over had completed 4 years of college or more. That number had improved to 14.7% by 1998.

During that period, the number of Black males age 25 and over who had completed 4 years or more of college increased from 6.7% to 13.9%. The corresponding increase for Black females was 6.2% to 15.4%.

Source: U.S. Census Bureau, Statistical Abstract of the United States: 1999, Table No. 264

In 1998, African Americans 18 years old and over, who were year-round full-time workers with a bachelor's degree, had an average income of $36,190.

African Americans 18 years old and over who were year-round full-time workers with high school diplomas only, had an average income of $24,055 (67% of the average income of bachelor's degree holders).

Source: U.S. Census Bureau, Money Income in the United States: 1998, P60 - 206

In 1990, the unemployment rate was 11.4% for Black Americans and 4.8% for Whites. The yearly unemployment rate for Blacks is typically more than double that for Whites.

As a result of the economic recovery that began in 1993, unemployment rates in 1999 fell to a 30 year low of 3.7% for White Americans, and a record low of 8% for Black Americans.

Source: Bureau of Labor Statistics Data, Labor Force Statistics from the Current Population Survey, January 2000 and earlier reports.

ECONOMIC CONDITIONS

Overall, economic conditions for Black Americans have shown improvement, but remain worse than for other major groups. A number of factors including educational attainment, employment status, family make-up, race, and lack of owner-ship of income-producing entities contribute to our scant economic circumstance. While it is clear that increasing educational attainment levels for Black Americans has had a positive impact on earnings, an expanding percentage of single-parent households continues to have a stifling effect on family income.

In 1998, 26.1% of Black persons lived below the poverty level. That figure was down from 30.8% in 1989.

Of all Black families, 23.4% lived below the poverty level in 1998. In 1989, that figure was 27.9%.

Source: U. S. Census Bureau, Poverty in the United States: 1998, Current Population Reports, P60-207

In 1998, the median* household income of Black Americans was lower than other major groups.

Asian and Pacific Islanders $46,637

White...$42,439

Hispanic..$28,330

African Americans $25,351

* The median is the value that divides the distribution into two equal parts, one half of the distribution exceeding the value, and one half below the value.

Source: U.S. Bureau of the Census, Current Population Survey, March 1999

In 1998, the median income of Black married-couple families was $47,382. That figure was 86% of the $54,845 median income of White married-couple families.

That year, the $17,737 median income of Black female householders with no spouse present was 64% of the $27,542 median income of their White counterparts.

Source: U.S. Census Bureau, Money Income in the United States: 1998, Current Population Reports, P60-206

More importantly, the $17,737 median income of Black female householders with no spouse present was only 37% of the $47,382 median income of Black married-couple families.

Clearly, the financial status of Black families is dramatically improved when our households are maintained by married couples.

Source: U.S. Census Bureau, Money Income in the United States: 1998, Current Population
         Reports, P60-206

OUR FAMILIES

The make-up of African-American families has changed in the last 30 years. Consistent with national trends, increased rates of divorce and separation, and the growing numbers of children born out of wedlock have accounted for more of our households being maintained by single women. The impact of these changes are evident in poverty rates for Blacks that are still more than double those for White Americans, despite an improved economy.

African-American households had an average of 3.7 members in 1980. By 1998, the average number of members per household decreased to 3.42 persons.

In 1970, 58% of all Black children lived in a two-parent household. By 1998, the number of Black children living in two-parent households decreased to 36%.

Sources: U.S. Census Bureau, Household and Family Characteristics: March 1998
U.S. Census Bureau, Current Population Reports, P20-514, and earlier reports.

In 1970, the proportion of births to unmarried African-American women was 38%. By 1998, that number had increased to 69%.

From 1991 to 1998, birth rates for Black teens 15 through 19 years old showed a 26% decline from 115 to 85.3 births per 1,000 women.

Sources: National Vital Statistics Report, Vol. 47, No. 25, October 5, 1999 and earlier reports.

From 1970 to 1998, the number of Black families headed by married couples decreased from 68% to 47%. Conversely, the number of single-parent families increased from 32% to 53% during that period.

In 1998, 8.6% of Black married-couple families lived below the poverty level. Among Black families headed by females with no husband present, 47.5% lived below the poverty level.

Sources: U.S. Census Bureau, Current Population reports, P20-515, and earlier reports.
U.S. Census Bureau, Poverty in the United States: 1998, Current Population Reports, P60-207

Author's Note

The troubling social problems that grip America as a whole have reached crisis proportions among young African Americans. We are witness to a generation decimated by violent crime, the accessibility of drugs, and a dangerous shift toward behaviors that have placed them at a high risk for failure. Certainly, there are many examples of those who avoid the obstacles and go on to lead productive lives, but it is painfully obvious that far too many are falling through the cracks. What can we do to improve their chances for success? The often-referred-to old African proverb that claims "It takes a whole village to raise a child" has merit. Customarily, adult members of the community are responsible for imparting the knowledge, the skills, and the behaviors that enable our young people to persevere. Whatever wisdom and understanding we have to offer cannot be successfully passed along without a strong community accord that assures the transference of that information. *Seeds of Success* was created for that purpose. For what may be the first time ever, we have a way to uniformly act on the message which the old proverb conveys. We cannot distance ourselves when so many of our young men, women, and children have become everyday casualties in a conflict that they are ill-equipped and unprepared to engage—life. We cannot be detached, knowing that their weaknesses are our weaknesses, their failures are our failures, and their inability to thrive: a telling reflection of our diminished efforts to provide them with the instructions necessary to survive in what has become an increasingly perilous environment.

Clearly, we cannot continue to look beyond the bounds of our own communities for the answers. Broad-based problems require broad-based solutions, and *Seeds of Success* affords us a rare opportunity to work collectively in passing on the power of positive influence. We owe it to ourselves and to future generations. No need could be more urgent, and no purpose more meaningful.

Vernon Arrington Jr.

*There are no self-made successes. Any one of us who
has experienced some measure of success in life can remember
the special people who gave the needed encouragement,
pivotal advice, or the direct assistance that made
all the difference in our lives. Seeds of Success
gives us that special ability to do the same for others.
Let's seize this opportunity.
Someday, when successful African-American
men and women reflect on their good fortune,
they will think of us, and be grateful that we were
there to make a difference in their lives.*

Seeds of Success

A Handbook for Young African Americans

Please send me _______ copies of *Seeds of Success* at $12.00 each plus $1.50 per book for postage and handling. New Jersey residents add 6% sales tax.

Name____ Phone (_______) _____________________

Address ____

City ____ State _______ Zip__________________

My check or money order for $__________ payable to The Deluge Press, is enclosed.
Mail to: The Deluge Press, P.O. Box 657, Egg Harbor, NJ 08215 - 0657

ASK ABOUT OUR QUANTITY DISCOUNTS (609) 965-7407

(cut or copy this form)

Order "Seeds of Success" today...
Join the fight for a better tomorrow.

Send orders to:
> The Deluge Press
> P.O. Box 657
> Egg Harbor, New Jersey
> 08215 - 0657

Your church or social group can make a difference by distributing Seeds of Success. For details, call The Deluge Press at (609) 965-7407.